MONICA'S
Untold
STORY

AN AMORALITY TALE

MONICA'S *Untold* STORY

AN AMORALITY TALE

BY ANONYMOUS

#1 Bestselling Author of *Humpty Dumpty*

ILLUSTRATIONS BY BILL PLYMPTON

ReganBooks

A Imprint of HarperCollins*Publishers*

PUBLISHER'S NOTE

As will be more than obvious to readers of this tale of shenanigans in places high and low, *Monica's Untold Story* is an unauthorized, unsponsored, unendorsed, fanciful comedic parody about the sorry public events of the past year.

Story by Anonymus. Text by Larry Amoros and Anonymus, with Marley Klaus and The Regan Company. Illustrations by Bill Plympton.

MONICA'S UNTOLD STORY. Copyright © 1999 by ReganBooks, Larry Amoros, and Marley Klaus. Illustrations Copyright © 1999 by Bill Plympton. All rights reserved. Printed in the United States of America. No part of this book may be used or reproduced in any manner whatsoever without written permission except in the case of brief quotations embodied in critical articles and reviews.
For information address HarperCollins Publishers, Inc., 10 East 53rd Street, New York, NY 10022.

HarperCollins books may be purchased for educational, business, or sales promotional use.
For information please write: Special Markets Department, HarperCollins Publishers, Inc.,
10 East 53rd Street, New York, NY 10022.

FIRST EDITION

Library of Congress Cataloging-in-Publication Data on file at the Library of Congress

ISBN 0-06-039303-3

97 98 99 00 01 10 9 8 7 6 5 4 3 2 1

Acknowledgments

This book could not have been written without the inspiration provided by every pig lawyer in America. Thank you.

This book is dedicated to Betty Currie.
We love you, Betty, because you're the only one
who didn't enjoy getting famous off of all this.

Please listen, dear friends,
to this unfolding tale,
Of power and lust
and greed and travail.

A story of clandestine
days and nights,
Of a starry-eyed girl
and her appetites.

Our saga begins in 90210—
That's Beverly Hills,
By now, we all know.

'Tis a town of implants
    and unwholesome deeds,
Where Visa and Amex
    can answer all needs.

A young girl needs love
   and care and protection.
But she should not grow up
   without discipline or direction.

Though appearing to live
   the American Dream,
Her parents would *spoil* her
   then fight, yell and scream!

In her pretty pink room
    did Monica hide,
Where she hugged all her dolls
    and cried, cried and cried.

She'd sit on her bed
    with her latest toy,
Yearning for what
She missed most,
    which was *joy*.

At first,
a nocturnal *sortie*
to the kitchen
Would ease her pain,
and relieve
all the itchin'.

This problem
her parents
could not ignore,
When they saw that
their daughter
had chewed thru'
the door!

So they gave their girl money,
   and off she went shopping.
At Bloomie's and Barney's
   the sales clerks were hopping.

Yet whatever she spent,
   there was still something missing.
She needed some goodness,
   which meant more than kissing.

Since the mall and the fridge
      had both failed to reach her,
She hatched a new plan
      to win over her Teacher.

She did extra credit
      with zeal near berserk,
And she went extra miles
      when presenting her work.

But her schoolgirl crush
   got way out of hand,
And a sordid affair
   with her Teacher began.

When his wife found them out,
   she was sent on her way.
Monica was perplexed.
   "Do I still get an 'A'?"

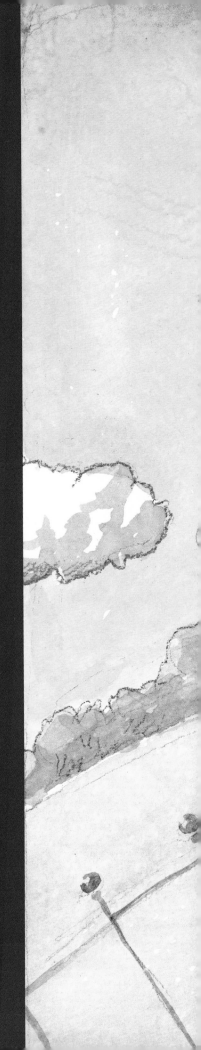

"The fling with my Teacher
    was full of despair.
It's making me think
    that I just shouldn't care.

"I see in my future
    a powerful man.
I'll lick him all over,
    THAT'S MY NEW PLAN!!!"

So off to D.C.
　　our heroine tramped.
A suite in the Watergate
　　is where she encamped.

Quite by chance,
　　and with no ounce of shame,
On these walls
In the White House
　　she'd soon leave *her* name.

In the grand Oval Office
    she found her soul mate,
The man of her dreams,
    her most perfect date.
"A man and a desk
    and a mountain of chow,
THIS IS FOR ME!
    I WANT IT ALL *NOW!*"

With a snap of her thong,
    and a pizza in hand,
A cigar in her mouth,
    on his lap she did land.

As she'd read in her *Cosmo*,
    she thought she was set.
He looked down her blouse
    and he called her *"my pet."*

In an instant
she knew
that she'd
be his
for life.
*So what
if he had
a kid and
a wife?*

She played
fallen Scarlett
to his
swashbuckling
Rhett.
For the rest
of her life,
she would be
his *coquette*.

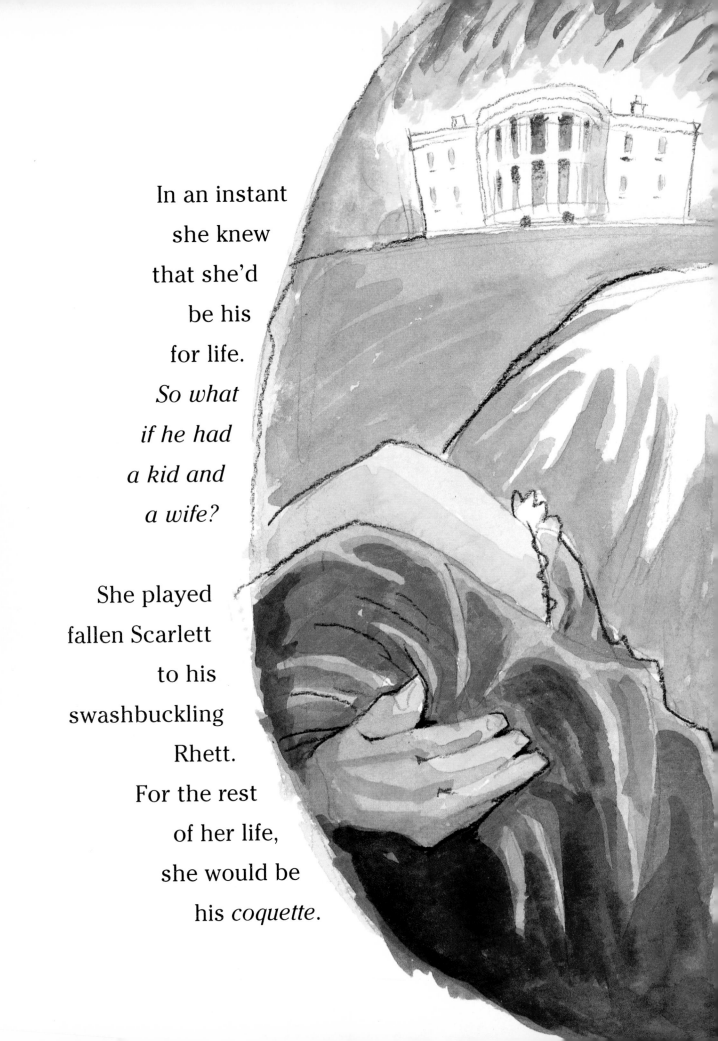

At night
She'd go home
   to Ben and to Jerry,
And savor the flavor
   of a Garcia named Cherry.

He'd call her to say
   that he wanted to *groan,*
And she'd whisper sweet nothings
   into the phone.

From her heart
And her soul
   she had so much to say . . .

But she needed
That Hillary
   out of the way!!!

As The First Lady's downfall
went thru' her head,
She heard these four words,
left better unsaid . . .

Paula!

Eleanor!

Gennifer!

Kathleen!

"To him I'm a *mule*—
Just part of a team."

"I'm your *only* true friend!" said one Linda Tripp. "Don't let him hurt you, don't you dare flip!

"You must hold
your head high,
have grace and
be proud.
Now kindly
speak up
in a voice that is
LOUD!"

But unknown to Monica,
    a dark storm was brewin',
A black cloud in D.C.,
    an omen of *ruin*.

A rattling of skeletons,
    a shaking of bones,
Begun by a trailer-park honey
    named Jones.

She would soon meet up
    with a lawyer named Starr,
Who would threaten and hound her,
    with feather and tar.

"Why, Truth and Justice
    are *all* that I seek!
You don't mind,
    Girlfriend,
If I take a quick peek?!"

unknown
animal
matter

Godiva
chocolate

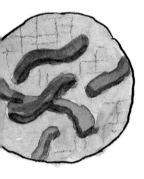

residential
sweat

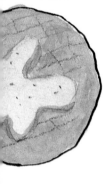

mozzarella
cheese

"It's not my intent
to shake you with fear.
It's simply my job to
Sniff,
Snoop,
and Leer.

"It's Billy Boy, *That Sex Hound,*
who made this sick mess.
So *damn it,* you wench,
HAND OVER THAT DRESS!!!"

She sensed all the rumblings
    that were sure to come soon.
The Congressmen bayed,
    like wolves at the moon.

From Blumenthal to Barr
    and all thru' The House,
Every creature would stir,
    every pollster and louse.

"I didn't have sex with *That Woman,*" he preached. . .

　to all of America in a televised speech.

But a t-shirt,

　some chocolates,

　a dress,

　and a tie,

Served as telltale reminders

　of his sad, twisted lie.

As Betty hid gifts

　safe out of sight,

The pundits came screaming

　from the left and the right.

Geraldo

    and Carville

    and Dershowitz, too

The talking heads talked,

    'Til they talked themselves blue.

        As Cokie and Sam

           both screamed from afar,

        "He gave a pin to a fat girl!

           Calm Down!" quipped Bill Maher.

But for now, all was calm.
    Bill read *Leaves of Grass*,
And thought how he'd soon miss
    this fine piece of ass.

The Intern was happy
    to neck in his castle,
Clueless
He wanted her dumped,
    without hassle.

Like THAT
She was picked up
    and tossed from his bed,
Yet thoughts of her lover
    remained in her head.

As she walked through the Pentagon
    admiring each missile,
She dreamed of her Bill,
    and of whetting his whistle.

"WAG THE DOG! WAG THE DOG!
    GO BOMB IRAQ!
I KNOW THAT SOMEDAY
    MY DEAR BILL WILL COME BACK!!!"

She stood by her man,
    feeling his pain.
Yet just two days later,
    she was off in a plane.

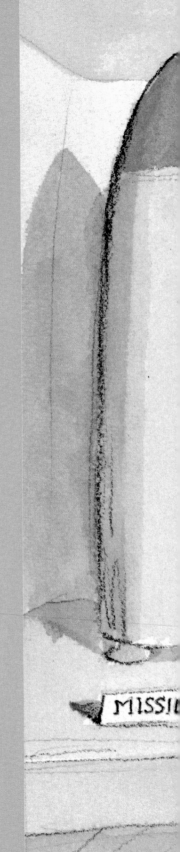

"I *suggest* that you leave,"
    said Vernon that day,
"And you must go now,
    and go far, far away!!!"

"BUT I WANT TO STAY PUT!
    TAKE YOUR HANDS OFF OF ME!!!
You know what you are?
    YOU'RE AN OLD *F.O.B.!!!*"

"So *love* doesn't matter,"
she wept to herself,
"And *goodness* and *truth*
can go back on the shelf."

As she soared to new heights,
her heart was a-breakin',
But that would soon change,
her own spin, she was makin'.

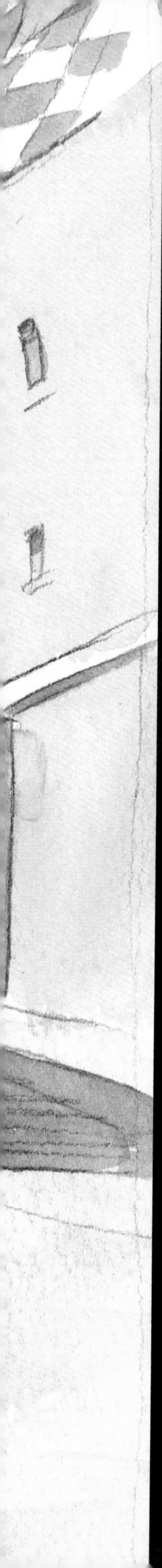

"I'll start a new life!
I've got a new plan!
I'll make lots of deals!

TO
HELL
WITH
THAT
MAN!

Manhattan's my town,
with restaurants galore!
Show me the money!
I WANT MORE AND
MORE!"

"For *Vanity Fair*
    I'll pose like Monroe,
The beauty who fell
    so far and so low.

"As for me,
I can handle the fame
    and the glamour.
Make the damn press
    all *beg*, *fawn* and *clamor*."

'Twas ABC's Barbara
    who captured the claim,
To sit with poor Monica
    and clear her bad name.

"I never knew that it was wrong,
    to dance and prance and flash my thong.
There was no sex," again she lied.
    "I like to knit!" she said, then cried.

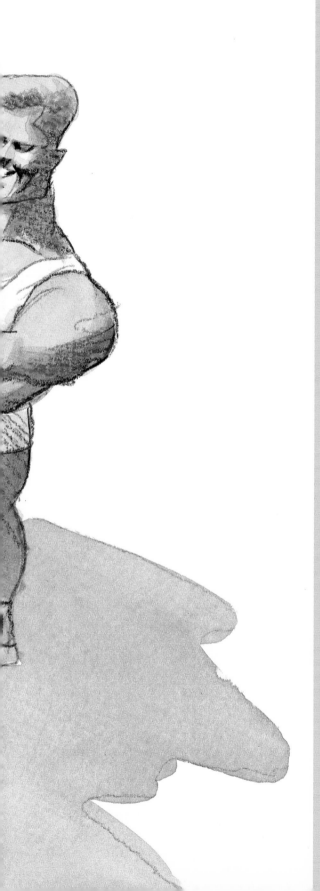

But crying
    did not stop The Beast,
That dwelled within
    and made her feast.

She feasted and indulged
    each vice.
"You get *nothing*,
    I've learned,
    just from being nice!"

Tho' Monica believed
    that her future was made,
She'd become a *cartoon*
    in life's cruel parade.

Hovering high
    through the streets of the city,
"'Tis a pity," she thought,
    "that this life's not so pretty."

From the top of the world,
   she took one more bite.
It's tragic, but this
   was the end of her fight.

For fortune and fame
   were not all that they seemed,
And a life without virtue
   was hard to redeem.

Her days now are spent
    all frozen in sight,
Of those who pursue her
    and flash her with light.

For the rest of her days
    she'll be known as the one
Whose amoral acts
    no longer seemed fun.

    The lessons she learned
        came at a price:
    To sin without shame
        is *really* not nice.

So Remember . . .

When grace turns to Envy, and kindness to Wrath,

you're steering your fate down a dangerous path.

When Sloth, Pride and Gluttony take hold of your life,

your future is darkened by sadness and strife.

With Greed, there's no giving which makes life divine.

So it's time you stop thinking that "Everything's mine!"

And Lust without Love will damage your soul.

(This, by the way, is not something to poll.)

So remember this tale of now-tarnished glory,

and heed the grim lesson of Monica's story:

If you should decide to lie and to cheat,

    there's only one person whom you'll <u>never</u> beat.

That someone is you—for way deep inside,

    from which there is nothing that you'll ever hide,

There'll be a sad, lonely and cynical you

    With a soul all black, and a heart all blue.

So no matter how tempting, you mustn't choose sin,

    for with goodness and grace, in the end, you will win.

The End

Bill Plympton is best known for his animated short films, including the Oscar-nominated *Your Face* and the Cannes Prix du Jury winner, *Push Comes to Shove.* His cartoons are a staple at animation festivals and on MTV, and his animated feature *I Married a Strange Person* is in current release through Lion's Gate Films. His illustrations have graced the pages of *The New York Times*, *Vogue*, *Rolling Stone*, *Vanity Fair*, and others. He lives in New York City.

Anonymous is the #1 bestselling author of *Humpty Dumpty.* He resides in 90210.

Visit Bill Plympton at his official website, www.awn.com/plympton/.